ESCAPE ROOM

Can You Escape the Museum?

HOW TO PLAY

Are you ready to escape the museum?

In a moment you'll turn the page to begin your adventure,
but first, here's how to play . . .

As you follow the story through the book, you'll find a series of mind-boggling puzzles. To solve each one you'll need to use pressed-out items from the paper sheets in the envelope inside the book. It's your job to work out which item you need for each puzzle.

If you get stuck, look at the hint card for that puzzle. There are three hints on each card. Turn the hint card around to read hint 1, which is on the back, and see if you can now solve the puzzle. If not, flip the card over to look at hint 2, and then, if you need to, turn it again to read hint 3. You can check your answers on page 48. Good luck!

Before you begin, take everything out of the envelope inside the book:

1. Find the two hint card sheets. Press out the cards and fold each one along the crease so that you see the front. Put them to one side as you play. Make sure you can't see the back of each card!

Press out
& fold!

2. The rest of the sheets contain items that you will use to solve the puzzles. Press them out as you make your way through the book. You'll need to fold some of them to make 3-D objects:

- Press them out carefully, pushing out any sections that have diagonal lines on them.
- Then fold them along the creases, folding away from you.
- Push the tabs into the slots to hold them together. The tabs and slots are labeled with letters to help you push the correct tabs into the correct slots—start with A and continue in alphabetical order.
- **Don't use tape—if you do, you won't be able to unfold and reuse the items.**

Press out
& build!

3. When you've finished playing, keep all your items safe in the envelope.

ESCAPE ROOM

Can You Escape the Museum?

Dr. Gareth Moore

Beatriz Castro

Kane Miller
A DIVISION OF EDC PUBLISHING

A MYSTERIOUS MESSAGE

It all started a few days ago when you received a strange letter.
You had no idea who it was from, but it was written by hand and
addressed to you. Inside was a map and a short message:

The museum needs your help.
February 29
8 p.m.

And now here you are. As the sun begins to set, you creep around
the edge of the museum building, following the instructions in your
hand. There it is: a small door set in an ivy-covered wall
that's marked "enter here" on the map.

You turn the handle, take a deep breath, and enter . . .

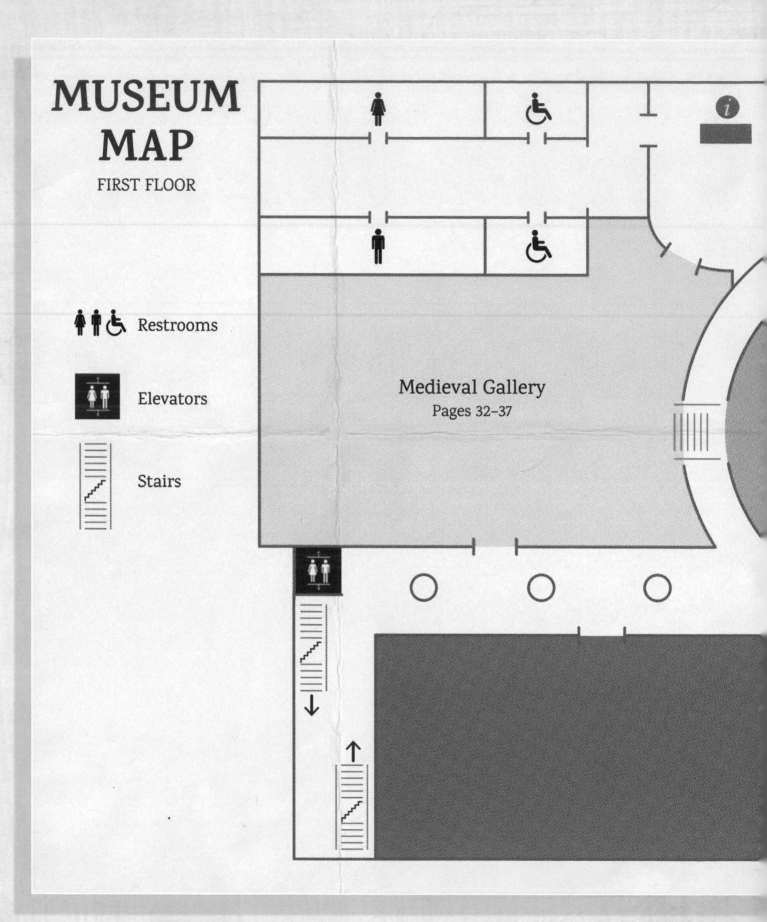

MUSEUM MAP

FIRST FLOOR

Restrooms

Elevators

Stairs

Medieval Gallery
Pages 32–37

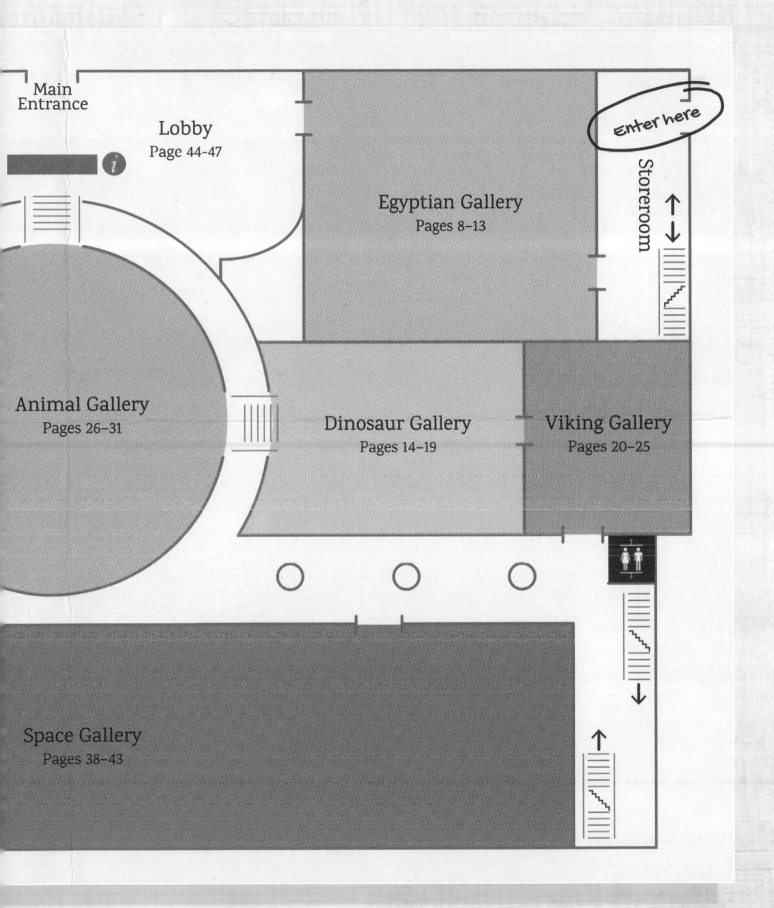

Main
Entrance

Lobby
Page 44-47

Enter here

Egyptian Gallery
Pages 8–13

Storeroom

Animal Gallery
Pages 26–31

Dinosaur Gallery
Pages 14–19

Viking Gallery
Pages 20–25

Space Gallery
Pages 38–43

TRAPPED IN THE
EGYPTIAN GALLERY

The door opens into a dusty storeroom. It's not somewhere you want to linger, so you pass through quickly and find yourself inside the Egyptian gallery. It's deserted. Moonlight casts large shadows across the floor and your footsteps echo. Why are you here?

Is that heavy breathing coming from behind the sarcophagus? Spooked, you try to leave, but none of the doors will budge. They're locked.

You'd better hurry up and work out how to escape.

You need to find a key to unlock the doors. Where could one be? Trying not to panic, you spot **a small wooden box** in one of the displays that rattles when you pick it up. Maybe there is a key inside.

There doesn't seem to be a way to open the box, but **a strange shape** is etched into the top, as if there are some pieces missing. **Is this some kind of puzzle?**

Stuck?
Your hint cards contain extra clues to help you figure out the puzzles.

The completed box reveals a word, but this only confuses you more.
How will a word help you escape? This museum trip is getting
stranger and stranger . . . As you mutter the word out loud you hear a
click as the box magically unlocks. But there's no key inside, just an
ancient piece of papyrus.

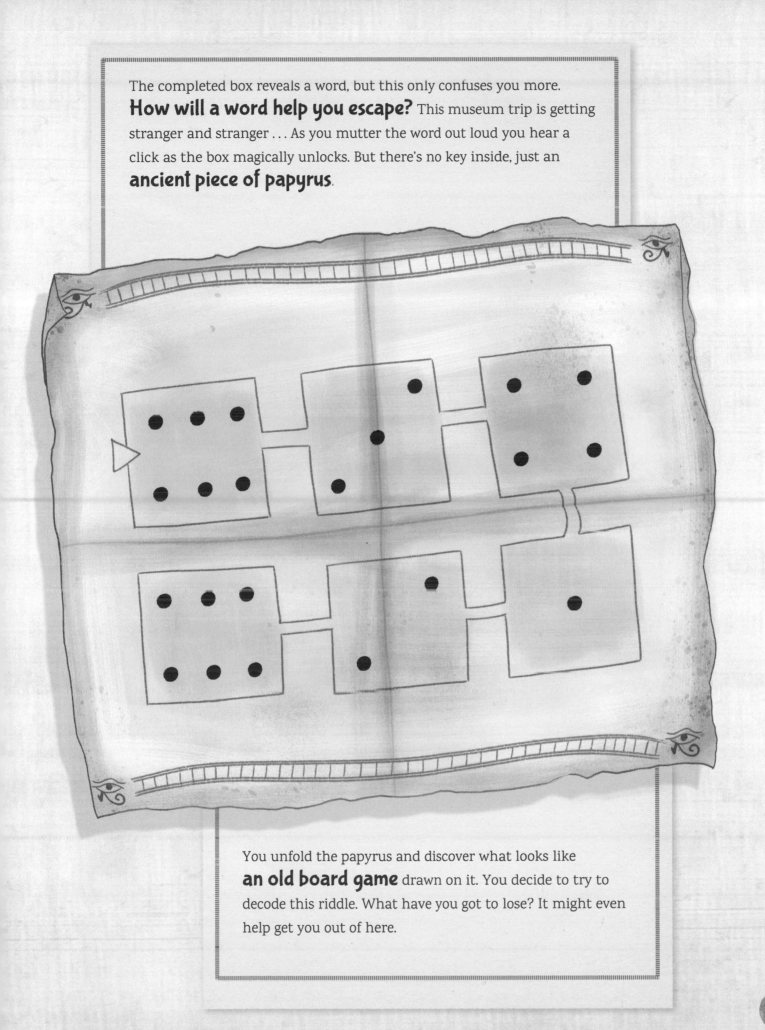

You unfold the papyrus and discover what looks like
an old board game drawn on it. You decide to try to
decode this riddle. What have you got to lose? It might even
help get you out of here.

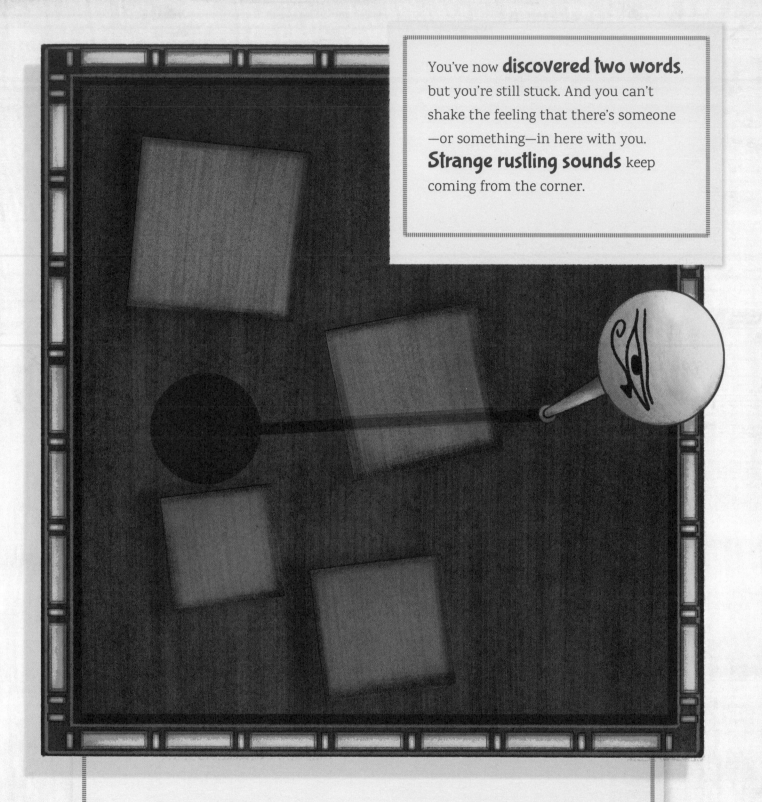

You've now **discovered two words**, but you're still stuck. And you can't shake the feeling that there's someone —or something—in here with you. **Strange rustling sounds** keep coming from the corner.

Just then, you see a familiar sign in the display case. The eye symbol that appeared on the papyrus is repeated on a **gleaming gold ball** that is mounted on a stick above a tray. On the tray are **four empty squares**, as if some items are missing. Should you try to return the lost objects to their rightful places?

Cartouche

Now you have collected three words. It's as if they should **spell out a message**, but it doesn't make sense. There must be more words to find.

Looking around the room, one sarcophagus stands out. The **label has been removed** from the base, as if someone is trying to **hide a name**.

Above the space where the label should be is a cartouche. Maybe that's the name in **hieroglyphics**—can you decode it?

Read once you've solved the puzzle.

Once you've cracked the cartouche code you have four words, which spell out a message. It must be referring to this sarcophagus. You hesitate for a second, but another loud sound startles you into action. Trembling, you **give the sarcophagus a push**. It slides across the floor to reveal some steps leading down into a tunnel. **You're free!**

LOCKED IN WITH
DINOSAURS

You emerge from the tunnel through a vent into . . .
oh, it's the dinosaur gallery. You haven't
escaped the museum after all.

You notice right away that some of the exhibits
seem to have been disturbed. There are bits of
dinosaur fossil lying around and it looks as if
something has been trying to eat them. You try
the exits, but they're locked. It's almost as if
someone wants to keep you inside this museum.

Frustrated, you gaze around. At the far end of the gallery, in front of one of the display cases, a **screen is flashing**. When you get closer, you see that the exhibit has been damaged. All that remains are some **footprints in the sand**.

The screen stops flashing and changes to display a question. Can you answer it?

WHICH DINOSAUR DOES NOT BELONG HERE?

BRACHYLOPHOSAURUS

STEGOSAURUS

CENTROSAURUS

PROTOCERATOPS

As you press the correct dinosaur, another screen starts blinking across the room, next to a **large stegosaurus model**. A light comes on, illuminating its foot. But again, it's damaged, and the **toes are missing**.

The flashing screen shows a keypad with the numbers 0 to 9, and it asks a question: **"In what order do I tread?"** If you can discover the answer, you might be one step closer to getting out of here.

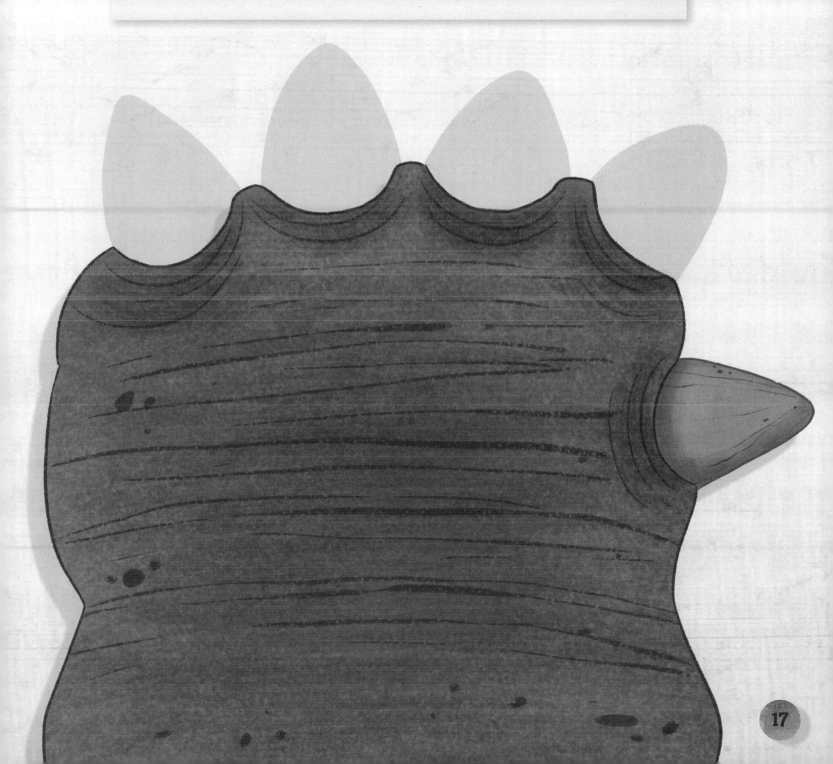

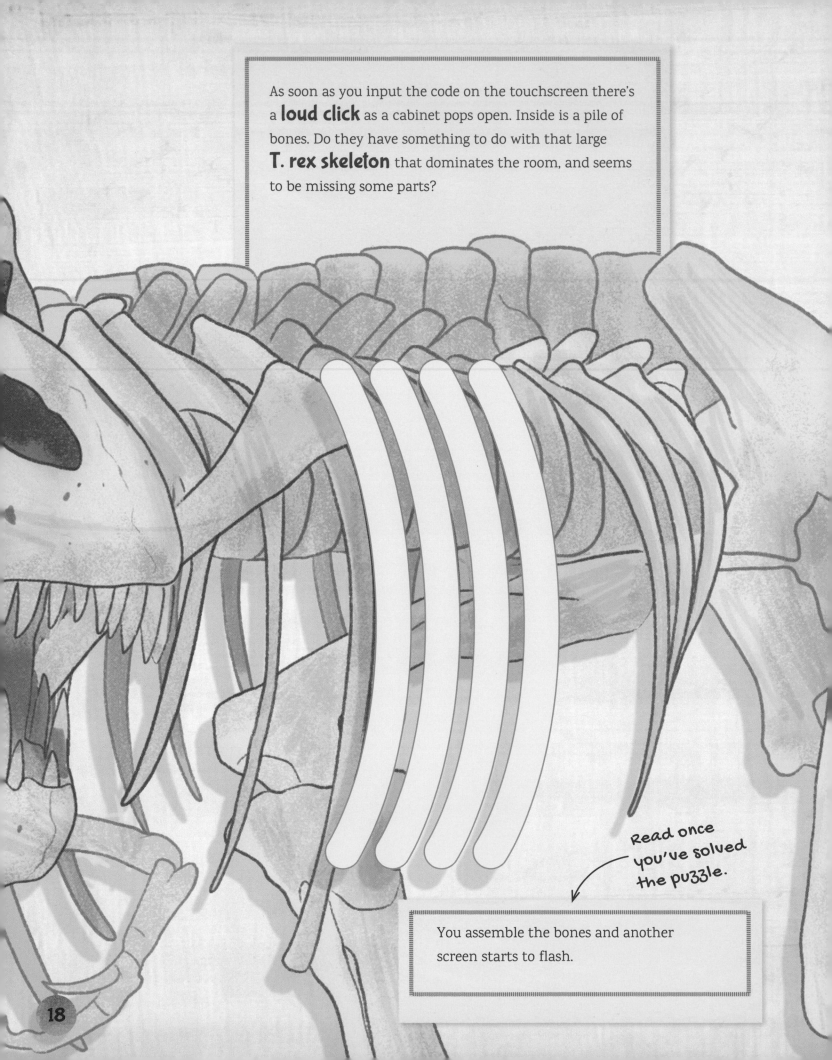

As soon as you input the code on the touchscreen there's a **loud click** as a cabinet pops open. Inside is a pile of bones. Do they have something to do with that large **T. rex skeleton** that dominates the room, and seems to be missing some parts?

Read once you've solved the puzzle.

You assemble the bones and another screen starts to flash.

Next to the screen you see an **empty dinosaur's nest** with some **letters written around the edge**. Can you put the missing items back into the nest and discover a hidden message?

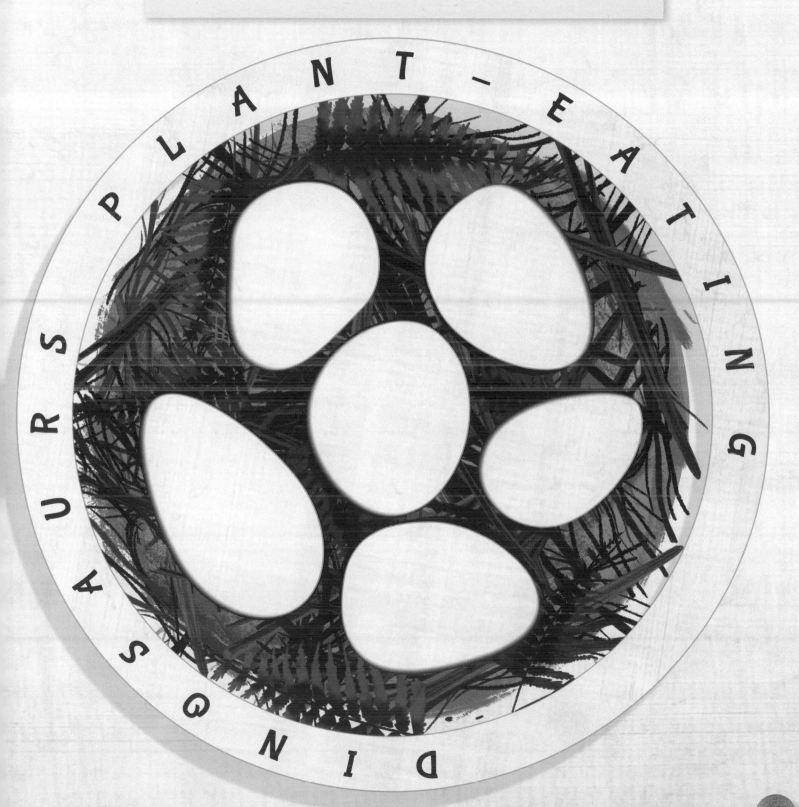

PLANT-EATING DINOSAURS

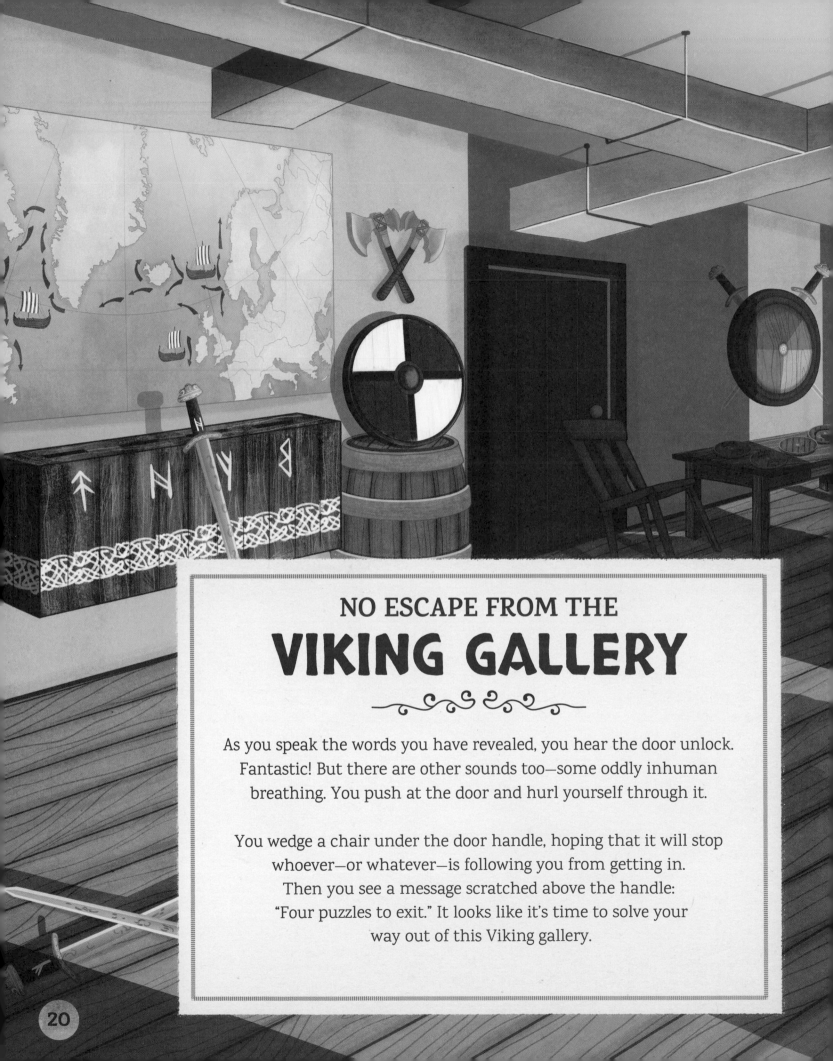

NO ESCAPE FROM THE
VIKING GALLERY

As you speak the words you have revealed, you hear the door unlock.
Fantastic! But there are other sounds too—some oddly inhuman
breathing. You push at the door and hurl yourself through it.

You wedge a chair under the door handle, hoping that it will stop
whoever—or whatever—is following you from getting in.
Then you see a message scratched above the handle:
"Four puzzles to exit." It looks like it's time to solve your
way out of this Viking gallery.

In the center of the room is a case full of intricate **Viking brooches**. But there's something in the display that doesn't match the other items: it's a **gleaming silver disk** with letters **scratched around the edge**. What could they mean?

One puzzle down, three to go. The word you've discovered takes you over to a **rack of Viking weapons** on the wall, below a large map. But the weapons themselves seem to be missing.

Could the **missing weapons** help you work out where to look for the next puzzle, to escape this creepy place?

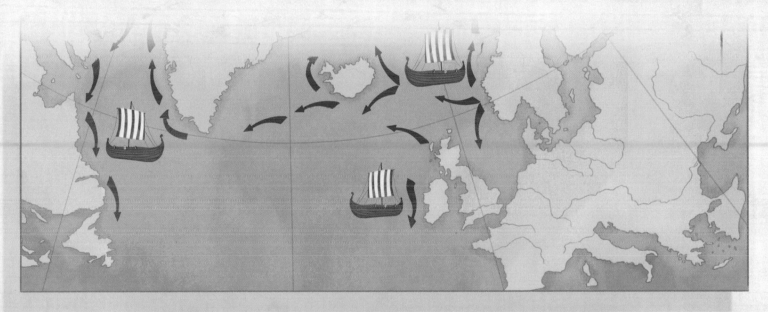

Of course, Vikings didn't just need weapons—they also needed armor. A few steps take you over to a display of **decorated Viking shields**. A "Make Your Own Shield" activity is set out on the table below it.

What should you do with the pieces? Can you **recreate the shield** that's displayed on the wall?

As you complete the shield, a set of spotlights turns on to light up a **dazzling display of jewels**, each in its own display box.

The jewels have **Viking runes** etched on them. On a piece of paper next to them is a chart that can be used to convert runes to modern letters.

It looks like you need to reveal a word in order to continue—but how?

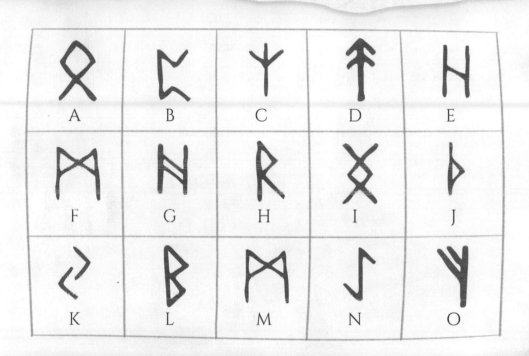

You've done it! The moment you reveal the answer the **far door swings open**. You glance at the door you came in through. Something is **rattling the handle**, but the chair is still keeping the door firmly shut . . . for now. Through the door you glimpse a corridor. Could this finally be the way to the museum exit?

Read once you've solved the puzzle.

CORNERED IN THE
ANIMAL GALLERY

Your footsteps echo as you run down the corridor. You try the handles on doors as you pass, but they're all locked. At last, a door swings open and you enter the animal exhibit, filled with large model animals. You'd head over to admire them were it not for the sudden loud bang you hear from behind you. You need to hurry!

The gallery is a complete mess! Whatever is in this museum with you has thrown things all over the place.

Lying on the floor in front of a display on animal cruelty are some **pictures of animals**. On closer inspection, you see a **shallow, empty cage** on the wall. Should one of the pictures go inside? Which one?

A crashing sound behind you makes you jump. Has your pursuer finally caught up with you?

Phew, they haven't yet—the noise was a display on honeybee hives collapsing. A **honeycomb model** has shattered into pieces, leaving the shape of where the **hexagons should be placed**. Can you put the pieces back?

Now that you've discovered two words, you're on the hunt for more! It must be another message. A large **bird migration display** seems to have been tinkered with. It's meant to show the routes that birds fly from south to north every year—but they are missing, and someone has **scribbled words** all over the map.

Can you **replace the routes** on the map? Does doing this reveal anything?

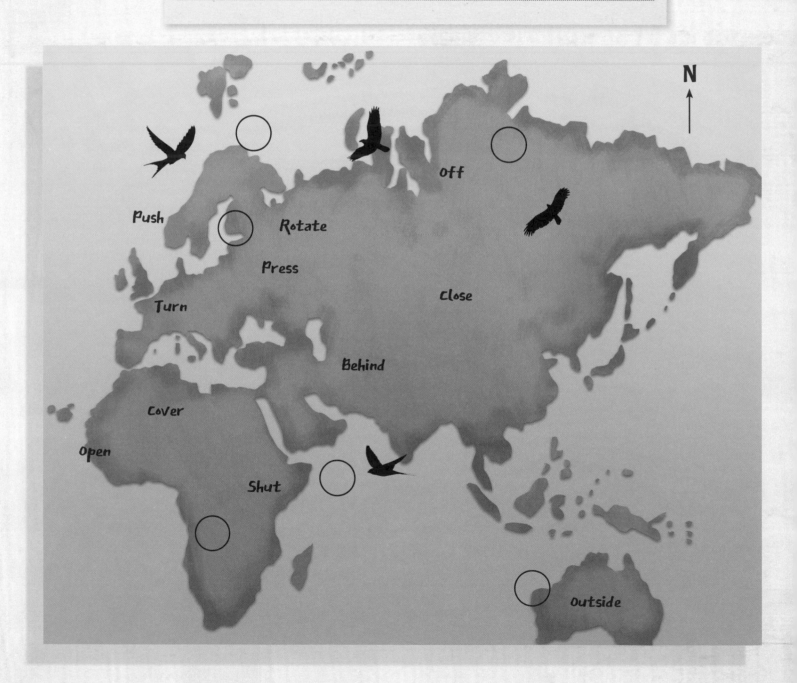

You've discovered one more word, and you're one step closer to understanding the message. Directly behind you is an **arachnid exhibit** that also seems to have been tampered with. Trapped in a **large spiderweb** aren't insects, as you'd expect, but **silver tokens**, each with a letter scratched into it. Another puzzle to solve!

Next to the web is a **picture of a spider**. Can you fit it on the web?

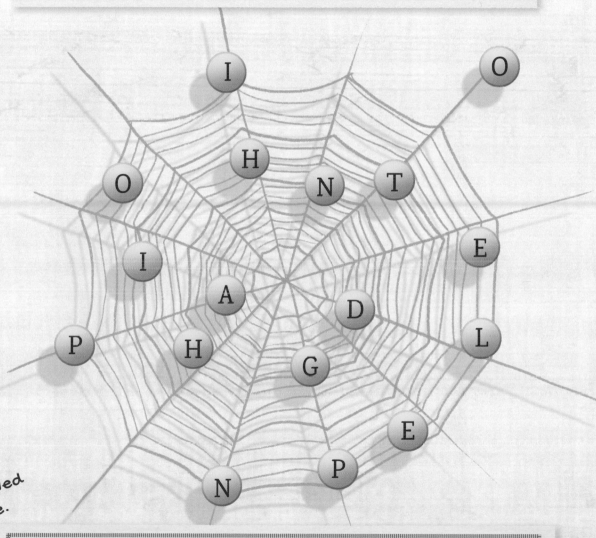

Read once you've solved the puzzle.

Success! The four words that you've revealed in this gallery explain **how to leave** the room. Following the instructions, you squeeze behind the model and see, as promised, **the way out**. Could you finally be **escaping the museum?**

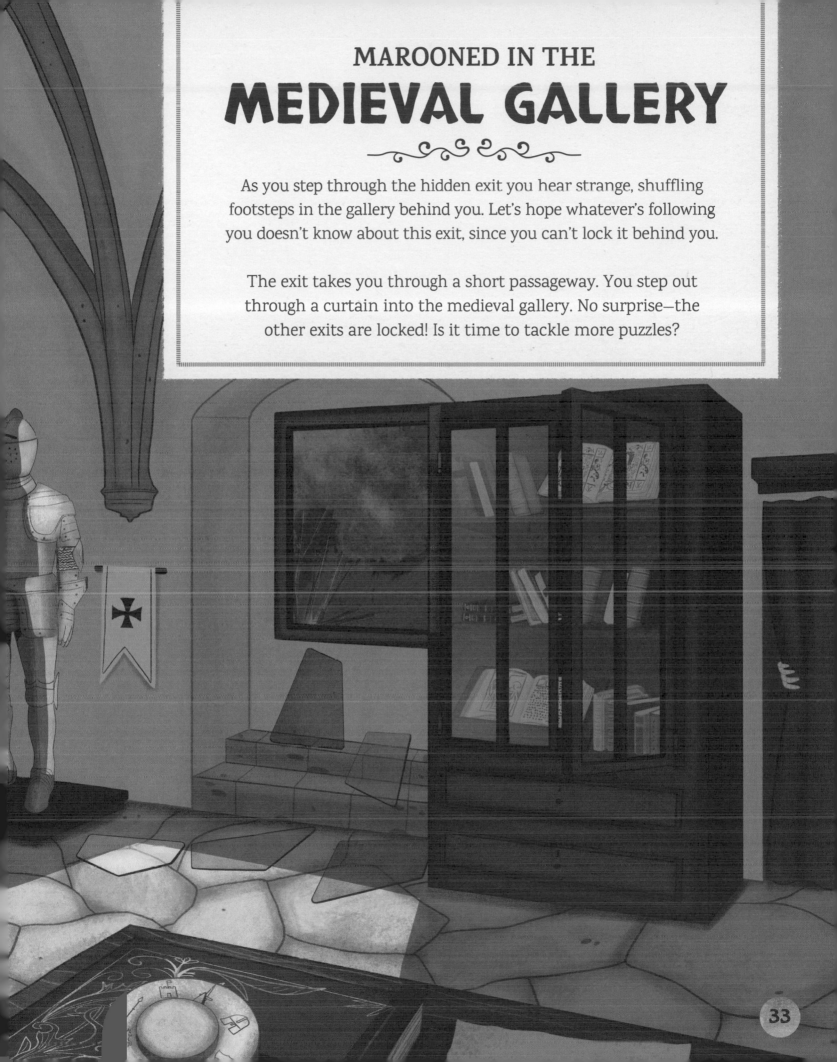

MAROONED IN THE
MEDIEVAL GALLERY

As you step through the hidden exit you hear strange, shuffling footsteps in the gallery behind you. Let's hope whatever's following you doesn't know about this exit, since you can't lock it behind you.

The exit takes you through a short passageway. You step out through a curtain into the medieval gallery. No surprise—the other exits are locked! Is it time to tackle more puzzles?

As you walk through the gallery to see which fiendish tasks have been set for you here, there's a crunch beneath your feet.

Five pieces of stained glass seem to have fallen out of a window frame. Can you **place them back** into the frame?

The **footsteps in the passage** seem to be getting nearer. You step backward nervously, away from the curtain, and accidentally bump into a model castle. You turn around, hoping you haven't damaged it. There are **strange letters** scribbled along the top of one of the towers.

Pieces of the model are scattered on the floor, also with letters written on them. What do they mean? Can you try to **rebuild the top of the tower?**

The word you discover doesn't help you out of the gallery, but it does direct you to another display. An **ancient-looking book** is sitting on the table. It is held shut with a strange lock that seems to require a **series of symbols** to open it. Which four symbols do you need to unlock it?

Written on a scrap of paper beside the book are the following words. Are they a clue? What pages do they refer to? Is there a codebook somewhere?

Page 8, Page 3, Page 4, Page 2

The **lock clicks open** as you dial in the correct symbols. Lying on the first page is a key—but it's too small to open the exit door. Perhaps it opens the drawer beneath this table? It does!

In the drawer you find a **decorated wooden box** with a date carved on top. You shake it, and hear something inside. It's locked with a combination lock. You need a series of **four shapes** to open it. But what shapes do you need, and in what order?

The box opens and yes, there is a key inside. This time it fits the exit door! You struggle to turn it, but after a minute that feels like an hour you hear the **satisfying sound of the lock opening**.

You pass through the door and try to lock it behind you, but you cannot get the key to turn again. And you're sure you've just seen a hand starting to draw back the curtain . . .

Read once you've solved the puzzle.

STUCK IN THE
SPACE GALLERY

You cross the corridor and slip through a door that's ajar.
You are now in the museum's newest gallery: Space. You try
the tall exit doors on the opposite side of the cavernous room,
but as you expect, they're locked. This time, someone has placed
a strange-looking combination lock on the door, which requires
four four-digit codes to unlock it.

Each of the codes has a picture next to it. You spot the solar
system, the Moon, some constellations, and a rocket ship.
Time to get to work!

First up is the solar system display, and you're not surprised to see it's been tampered with: **the planets are missing**. You can see the pins where the planets should fit, and **sets of numbers** have been scribbled all over it.

If you can **restore the planets**, maybe you'll be able to **find the first code** to enter into the lock on the door.

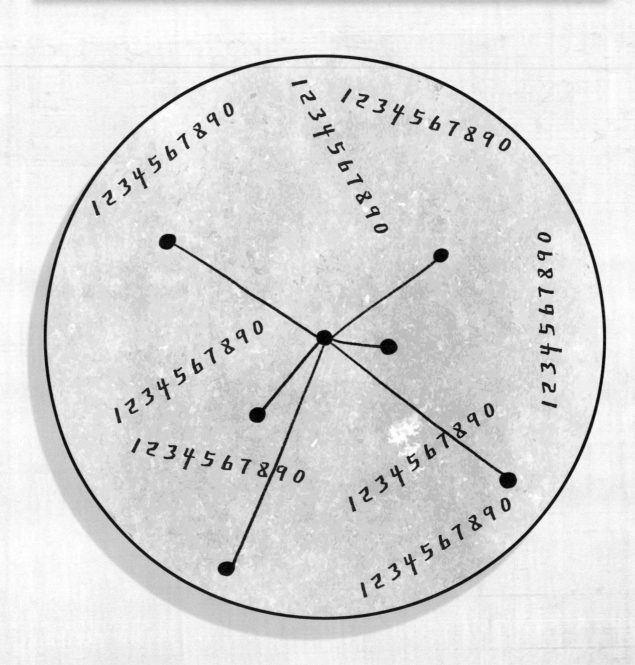

The second puzzle you tackle is the Moon exhibit. You try to stay calm, but you're sure that you can hear a **groaning sound coming from the lunar module** at the far end of the room. Come on, focus!

A chart shows the **phases of the Moon**—but you know you need a four-digit number to enter into the lock. How can you get one?

Another noise. That one was definitely not your imagination. Out of the corner of your eye you spot movement. **You need to act quickly**. The next picture on the combination lock is of constellations.

You dash over to the large star display and stare at it. All you can hear now is your own panicked breathing. There's a **sign pinned to the display—** and you feel fairly certain it is not part of the normal exhibit. **Part of it has been torn off**. Can you find the rest of it?

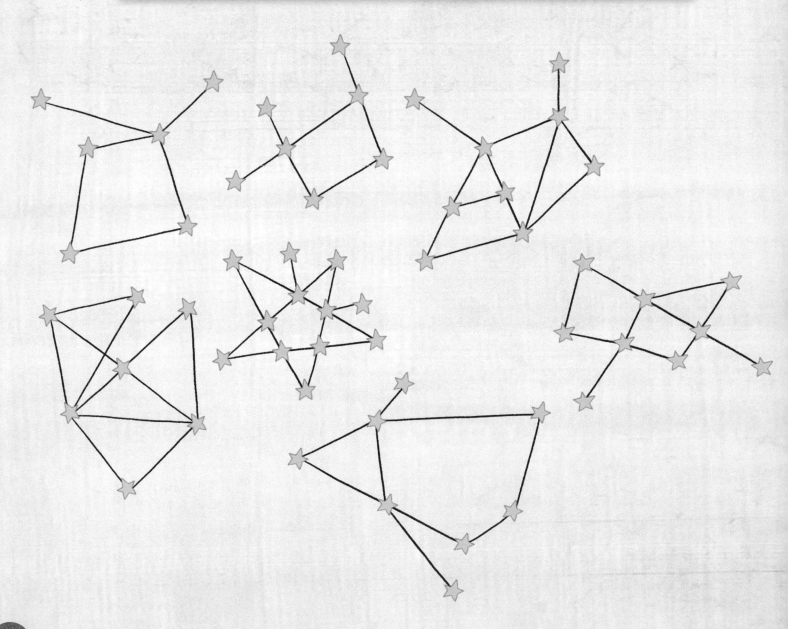

Just one final four-digit number and you're out of this room! The lock shows a **picture of a rocket ship**—but where is it? There are no rockets matching the image in this gallery.

Then you hear a rustle underfoot. There's a **crumpled piece of paper** on the floor, with a picture drawn on it. How is that supposed to help? Do you have to **build the rocket yourself?**

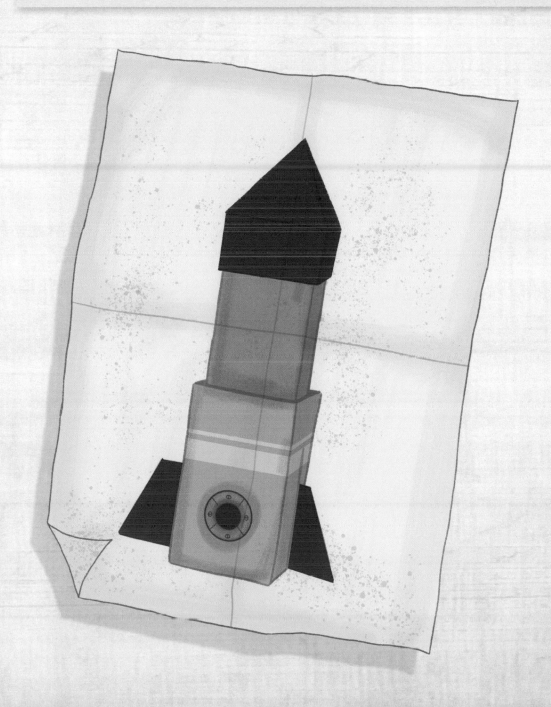

You sprint to the door panel to punch in the codes. Out of the corner of your eye you catch sight of a shabby, bandaged creature standing where you first entered the room. **Is it a mummy . . . come to life?** You enter the codes as fast as you can, and hear the door click open—but just before you can open it, **you feel a hand on your shoulder!**

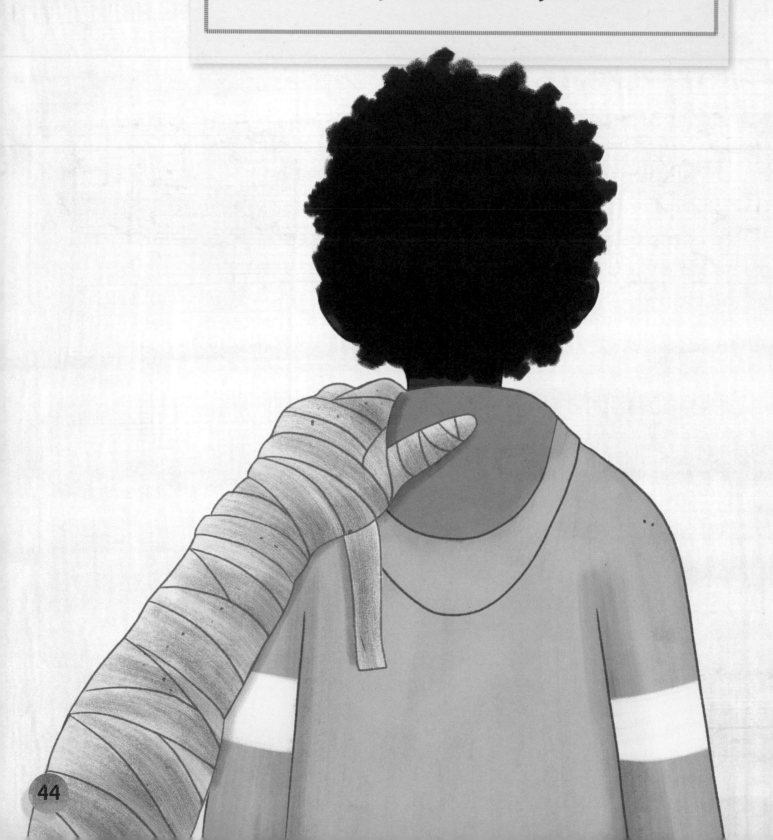

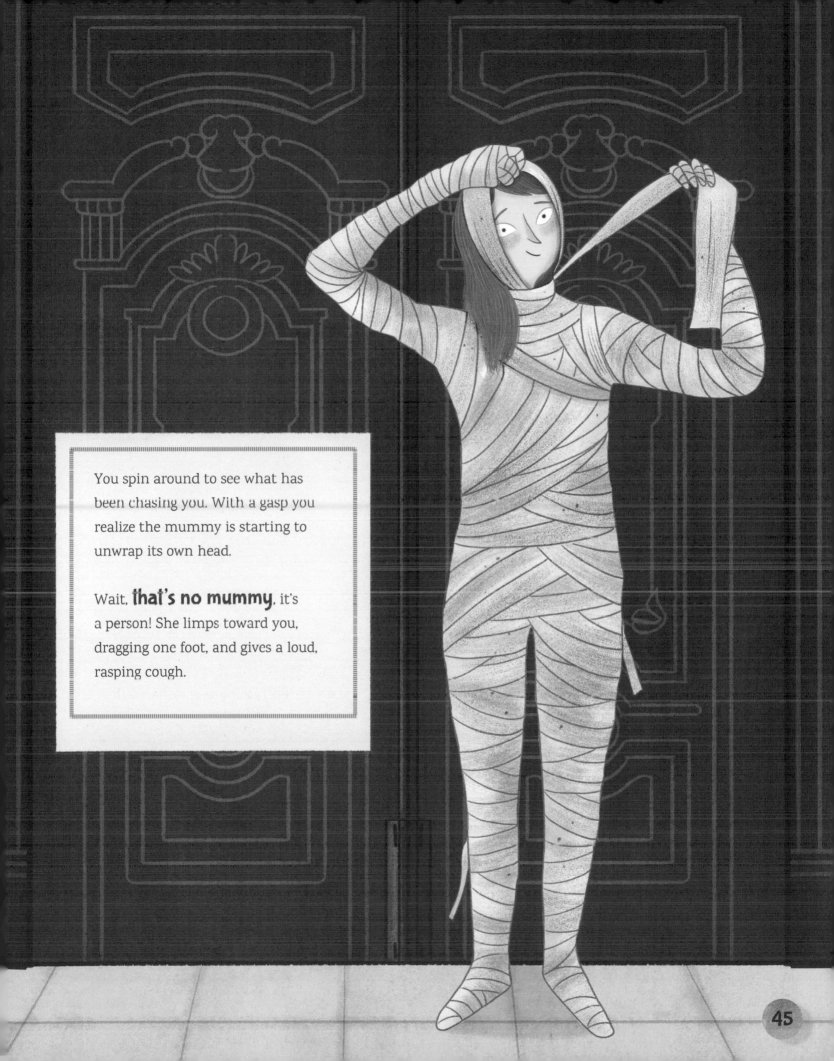

You spin around to see what has been chasing you. With a gasp you realize the mummy is starting to unwrap its own head.

Wait, **that's no mummy**, it's a person! She limps toward you, dragging one foot, and gives a loud, rasping cough.

Then she opens her mouth, and speaks in a perfectly normal voice:

"Sorry about that. Bit of a tickly throat. It's impossible to walk in this costume. But congratulations. You've passed the test.

Welcome to the League of Museum Guardians. You won't have heard of us before—we are top secret. Our mission is to defend museums around the world when they are faced with danger.

This medallion will let you know when the League needs you. Make sure you answer its call.

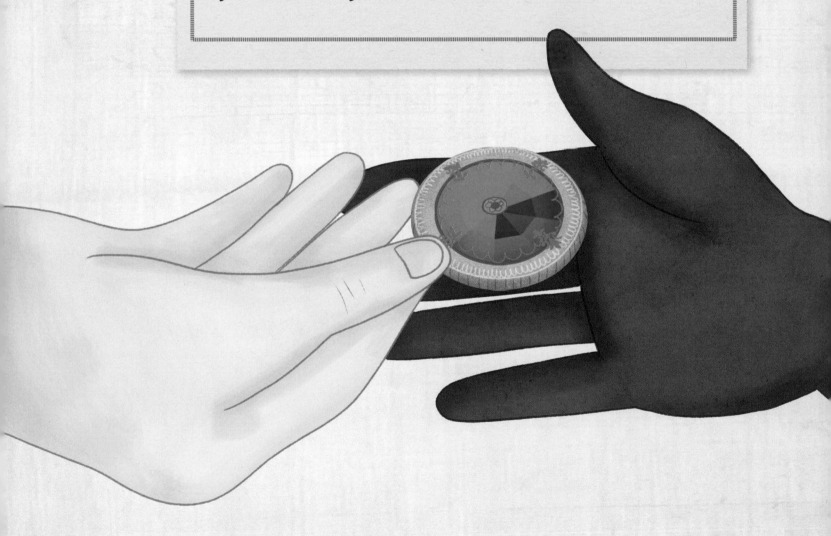

First American Edition 2021
Kane Miller, A Division of EDC Publishing

First published in 2020 by Welbeck Children's Books, an imprint of Welbeck Children's Limited, part of Welbeck Publishing Group, 20 Mortimer Street, London W1T 3JW.

Text & Illustrations © 2020 Welbeck Children's Limited, part of Welbeck Publishing Group.

For information contact:
Kane Miller, A Division of EDC Publishing
5402 S 122nd E Ave
Tulsa, OK 74146

www.kanemiller.com
www.myubam.com

Library of Congress Control Number: 2020939518

Printed in China
10 9 8 7 6 5 4 3 2

Story, text, puzzles and models written and designed by Dr. Gareth Moore
Commissioning Editor: Bryony Davies
Managing Art Editor: Matt Drew
Designers: Matt Drew & RockJaw Creative
Production: Nicola Davey & Gary Hayes

ISBN: 978-1-68464-226-7

Answers

Page 10: WARNING

Page 11: Place the dice so that the side that is facedown matches the number shown on the papyrus, then read the letters on the side that is now facing upward. The answer is ESCAPE.

Page 12: Place the pyramids on the squares so the shaded sides face away from the eye, to match the light, then look at them from the point of view of the eye to read BENEATH.

BE NE AT H

Page 13: Assemble the box with KING and NAME written on it, then slide the three cartouches into it so that they match the cartouche shown on the page. Next, turn them over and read the name of the king: RAMESES. The entire message reads: Warning, escape beneath Rameses.

Page 16: The stegosaurus' footprints don't fit, so it doesn't belong.

Page 17: Place the missing claws onto the page so that they fit exactly. Then turn them over and read the code: 2014.

Page 18:

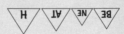

Page 19: Place the page onto the six eggs so that they fit exactly into the outlines shown. Next, trace a line from each arrow to the letter it points to at the edge. Finally, read these letters in order of the numbers marked on the eggs. This gives: OPEN UP.

Page 22: Place the brooch onto the page, aligning the cutout in the center with the hexagon shown. Rotate until you can read a word clockwise around the shape, starting from the top of the page. It reads: SWORDS.

Page 23: Assemble the cabinet shown in the picture, then insert the four swords into it so that the symbols on their handles match the symbols shown. Next, look at the letters on the parts of the swords that stick out from the bottom of the rack. You see the word SHIELDS.

Page 24: Stack the shield pieces in the following order: blue, yellow, green, red.

Page 25: Assemble the box and jewel shown, then rotate the jewel until the pattern on it exactly matches the pattern on the box. Now read the rune above number 1, and look up the letter in the table on the page. Repeat for 2, 3, and 4. Together, they spell GOLD.

Page 28: Assemble the cage. Placing the chimpanzee card in the cage reveals the word HIDDEN.

Page 29: Place the pieces so that EXIT is spelled across the shaded pieces, as shown.

Page 30: The word BEHIND is in the center of the migration routes.

Page 31: Place the spider so each of its feet exactly covers a letter. Then, read those letters in order from 1 to 8. They spell: ELEPHANT. The entire message reads: Hidden exit behind elephant.

Page 34:

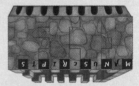

or

Page 35: The pieces reveal the word MANUSCRIPTS.

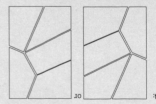

Page 36: Assemble the book by slotting the two pieces together. Make sure you place them so that you can then fold it in such a way that page 1 is at the front and page 8 is at the back, just like a real book. Now you can work out which is page 2, page 3 and so on. Use the page numbers to find the correct symbols. They are:

Page 37: Place the four panels so the holes reveal the date 1405. The shapes of the holes in the panels provide the code needed to unlock the box:

Page 40: Place the three black disks so that the planets line up with the circles, and you can see six black dots in the planet centers. Then read the number from left to right that is shown in the square cutouts. It reads: 5024.

Page 41: Stack the pieces in the order and orientation shown, so the full moon goes at the bottom and the smallest moon goes at the top. This reveals the code: 8347.

Page 42: The code is given by the number of stars in the constellations that could be drawn in a single, continuous line without tracing over any line more than once, ordered from smallest to largest: 6789.

Page 43: Assemble the rocket by building the nose cone (in red), the main body (with four numbers on it), the bottom section (with the circular windows), and the tail fin (with three numbers on it). Place the tail fin into the bottom section, then place the main body on top so it sits on the tail fin. Next, place the nose cone on top. Now you can read the four digits down the body of the rocket: 5237.